Holland

Fascinating Flowerfields

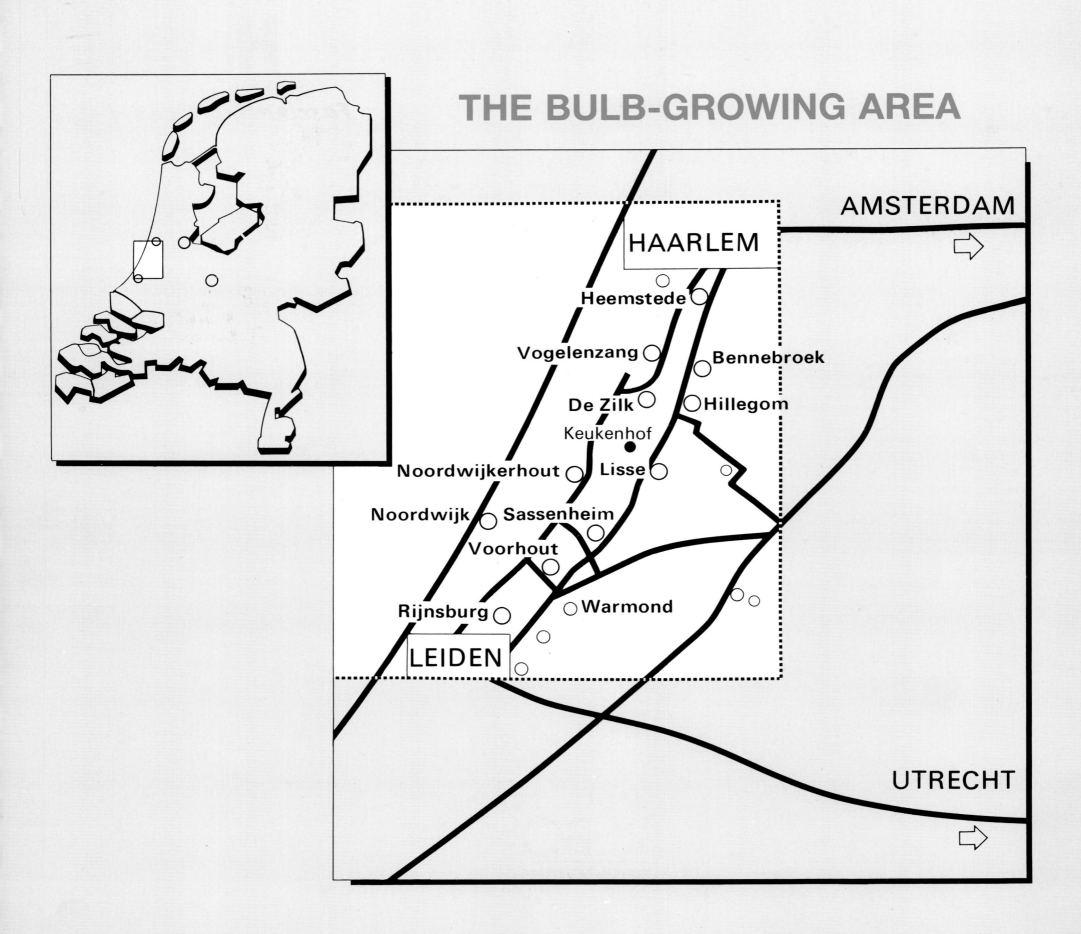

THE BULB-GROWING AREA

AMSTERDAM

HAARLEM

Heemstede

Vogelenzang

Bennebroek

De Zilk

Hillegom

Keukenhof

Noordwijkerhout

Lisse

Noordwijk

Sassenheim

Voorhout

Rijnsburg

Warmond

LEIDEN

UTRECHT

Holland
Fascinating Flowerfields

Herman van Amsterdam

Peter van der Voort

REBO
PRODUCTIONS

Welcome to Bulbland. The photographs in this book take you to the flat lands behind the Dutch dunes, known far and wide as the bulb-growing area. Every springtime anew, something magical happens here; it is the fairytale of thousands of bulbs blooming in the fields, which draws admirers from all over the world.

Tulips, hyacinths and narcissus; they blossom in thousands and colour the landschape in a wonderful way. The area where this spectacle of colour and fragrance is found, has some 100.000 inhabitants and lies hemmed in between the historical cities of Haarlem and Leiden. From the highest church towers, when the weather is clear, it is even possible to see the contours of the Dutch capital, Amsterdam.

The region where bulbs feel so at home, may certainly boast of a glorious past. What today is a pleasing springtime paradise of bulbs in flower, once was a wilderness with rough woods and treacherous swamps. A favourite territory of poachers and bands of thieves. The stage-coach made its way over the unpaved roads and the people were mainly farmers, who earned their living with their cattle.

The bulb may never have taken up such a prominent place in Holland had it not been for the horticulturalist, *Carolus Clusius*, who came here from Vienna, Austria in the 16th century. Clusius had to leave his home on the Blue Danube because of a religious dispute.

This renowned horticultural expert sought safety in Leiden, the university city on the Dutch coast. In his baggage were the tulip bulbs which had been given to him by an aristocratic friend from Turkey, the land from which the tulip originates.

It was in Leiden therefore that the four hundred year old history of the Dutch bulb-growing culture began. At first he rare tulip was an extremely luxurious item which only the very rich could afford.

Half way through the 17th century, it was quite normal for a single tulip to fetch a price of 5000 gulden. From that period, a trading transaction is

known where the following was paid for one tulip: 8 fat pigs, 2 loads of wheat, 5000 liters of wine, 1500 kilos of butter and 500 kilos of cheese. Phenomena which became known as 'tulipomania'. For a long time in Holland bulbs were also believed to have healing powers. In the 18th century especially, many pharmacists had bulbs amongst their range of products.

The hyacinth, for instance, was nicknamed 'the scare of the Arabs'. Its juice, mixed with half a glass of white wine was sold as a mixture to slow down beard-growth. There are also tales of the uses tulips were put to. It is said that it was customary in the courts of the French Sun King, Louis XIV (who was king from 1643 to 1715) for upper class ladies to adorn their decolleté with very pricey tulips instead of precious jewellery.

The tulip brought great riches but also poverty because in 1637 when the price of these colourful products plunged, thousands of speculators went bankrupt.

Nevertheless, the tulip had continued to appeal to the imagination and over the ages, had developed throughout the world into a favourite bloom with the Dutch bulb-growing region as the leading cultivation area.

Depending on the variety they belong to, the bulbs are planted in the months August, September and October and there they stay buried at a depth varying from about five to fifteen centimeters, for many months.

In earlier days, the planting was done by hand. Each bulb was neatly put into place in a row. Machines specially designed for the bulb-growing industry have in the meantime made manual work superfluous. Once the bulbs are beneath the earth, a layer of straw as thick as a quilt, protects them from frost. As soon as spring beckons, it is time to remove the winter blanket. The blooms then shyly push their slender stems up through the earth's crust and subsequently reach full development. Never is it possible to predict when the flowers will bloom. Every year

it is a matter of watching and waiting and things depend almost entirely on the weather conditions of the months preceding spring. A severe winter can delay blossom time while a mild December and January often hastens the process; the growers simply never know for sure. The capriciousness of the Dutch climate constantly contradicts every prediction.

Under normal circumstances -meaning a not too severe winter, no excessive rainfall- the bulb area usually bursts into colour around mid-March, in a consistent sequence of arrivals.

First come the crocuses (not a main variety but a sub-variety in the bulb growing industry). The yellow specimens come first, then the purple, the white and finally the lilac hues. In the meantime the first (mainly yellow) narcissus types announce themselves and simultaneously the hyacinths appear on the scene. The latter are meagre at first and have little colour but it only takes a few warm days for these same hyacinths magically to turn into robust clusters of red, pink, white or dark blue flowers.

As soon as the bulb region blossoms into colour, the interest manifested on the many by-roads which wind their way through the area, quickly mounts. This is not merely because of the things that wait to be seen; the fragrance produced by the flowers in the fields is sheer enjoyment too.

The hyacinths especially spread a sweet and transient scent which hangs like an invisible cloud above the land. What a delightfully relaxing experience it is peacefully to inhale the typical flowery perfumed air while admiring the multi-coloured palette.

The palette changes constantly. Once the hyacinths have blossomed, it is the tulips turn to demand attention and when it comes to colour variations, nothing can surpass them. Hundreds of different tulip types break into bloom. Short stemmed and long stemmed tulips; multi-coloured, small flowered or lavishly shaped tulips; early bloomers and late bloomers and a multitude of shades ranging from snow-white to almost black. Like all other bulb

families, the tulips stand in ranks in the fields. They are grouped in straight lines in beds which are approximately one meter wide and sometimes hundreds of meters long and separated from each other by narrow paths. Some colours are so vivid that they hurt the eyes if you look at them for too long.

By the time the long-stemmed Darwin tulips and late narcissus species bring the curtain down on this tempestuous festival of colour, it is mid May. The miracle is about to fade.

In the meantime the internationally known flower-parade has taken place in the region. This parade of floats, which draws hundreds of thousands of spectators, displays the products of the region in a unique way.

The first flower parade dates back to 1948 and since then never has a year been missed, no matter how bad the weather has sometimes been.

The floats which participate in the spring parade consist of a tractor understructure, over which a framework produced by blacksmiths and made of woven iron is fitted. Thatched mats are placed over the whole structure and on top of that, a carpet of flowers is planted, with enormous dedication. The finishing touches are brought about with bouquets and decorative silken cloths.

Accompanied by bands and dance groups, the floats which have taken thousands of hours of preparation, parade through the region along a route of some forty kilometers from Haarlem to the sea resort of Noordwijk.

Each year the parade has a theme; it could be a fairy-tale or titles like *Spring Parade*, *Fantasy and Reality* or something simple such as *'Lovely Holland'*.

The beauties of the region, dressed in romantic costumes, adorn the floats. The purpose of this free-for-all show is to introduce the products of the region to the public in a very special manner.

Incidentally, it is not only the flowers which draw the visitors to this little part of Holland. Touristically speaking, there are many other attractions.

The bulb-growing area includes Hillegom, Lisse,

Sassenheim, Noordwijk, Voorhout and Warmond. All these towns have enjoyed glorious histories of which many traces are still to be found.

For instance, there are traces of the Romans who at the beginning of the era built their settlements here. Also the terrible Normans - blonde hair, blue eyes and fearless of the devil himself - fought their battles here. Then, much later, in the Middle Ages the region became very popular with the nobility, many of whom chose this bulb-growing area to have country estates or castles built for themselves. There are many examples of these homes still to be seen, such as the beautifully restored Huys te Dever in Lisse, which was built around 1370.

In Sassenheim the well-conserved remains of the Teylingen castle (built around 1270) awakens memories of a distant past before there was even the slightest notion of a bulb industry and large hunting parties were organized in what was then merely a wild coastal area then.

Innumerable mansions and country estates have re-mained preserved for posterity. *Keukenhof*, once the herb and vegetable garden of the Countess of Holland, Jacoba van Beieren, is a fine example.

Immediately after the last World War, on the spot where this garden used to stand, a unique landscape architectural feat was accomplished. Here, not far from Keukenhof Castle, a garden was created, which has become famous throughout the world.

In *Keukenhof* myriads of variations of bulb-flowers have been brought together, alternating with lovely lakes, fountains, trees, shrubs and works of art. Around one million visitors come to Keukenhof every year to sample the profusion of flowers exhibited there.

There are many ways of enjoying the bulb-growing region during springtime. Cycling through the vast fields, driving along one of the many thoroughfares, wandering, or sitting comfortably behind a window in a touring couch; or from the air which provides yet a new perspective of the colour palette.

To give an impression of what the bulb region looks

like from the air, a number of aerial shots have been taken specially for this book. The pilot waited for days until the sky was more or less unclouded and the visability was good enough for the photographer to take these lovely bird's-eye view shots.

Their patience was sorely tried because the sort of weather conditions ideal for photographers, only occur sporadically in a Dutch springtime. What you see are unique photographs. The colour surfaces form brilliant patchworks in between townscapes, locks and canals. Some of the aerial photographs clearly illustrate the link between the North Sea, the dunes and the bulb fields.

The aeroplane went up again later in the year to record what the (colourless) bulb region looks like in wintertime. The locks and canals are frozen and the bulbs beneath the earth are covered with a warm blanket of straw.

The cultivation of bulbs has for a long time not been a strictly Dutch occupation anymore. In fact, the largest bulb field in the world is now in America.

In England, Spain, Italy, Portugal and Greece, there are a great many bulb growers. Japan even has 2500 nurseries, all based on the Dutch bulb-growing concept.

The Netherlands has a reputation to live up to in the field of bulb-growing. A great deal of know-how comes from this country and special machines are developed here which quietly take over all the manual labour. Right in the middle of the bulb growing region stands an internationally famous laboratory, where for decades knowledge has been assembled about bulb diseases, for instance. This knowledge finds its way to all countries where bulbs are cultivated; today there are ninety such countries. Yet nowhere in the world do the blossoming bulb fields present such a fantastic show as in that picturesque region, which fringes the Dutch dunes.

The zig-zag of hand-dug ditches form part of the bulb landscape. No longer do they serve as means of transportation, but they still play an important role in the smooth controlling of water so necessary for the cultivation of bulbs. In the springtime these ditches also provide an excellent opportunity to visit this area in the old-fashioned way: by canoe.

Not only is it a delight to behold the spectacular colour palette of the stretched-out fields; the whole area breathes a wonderful perfume, especially when the sweet-scented hyacinths bloom.
The numerous picturesque spots have been a constant source of inspiration for artists and photographers.

Nomatter how incredible it may sound, in the bulb area the flowers are merely an accessory. The bulb growers are primarily interested in the cultivation of healthy bulbs, which are subsequently exported or sold at local markets.

After a comparatively brief blossoming period, the flowers are 'beheaded' and even today this process is usually executed by hand. (Turn to the previous page for more information.) The final fate of the majority of flowers, is the trash-heap.

Only a small proportion of the flowers which decorate the fields, are destined for sale. Improvised wooden stalls pop up hither and thither in the bulb area during the flowering season (see photograph above).

The world's greatest garden, the Keukenhof in Lisse, beckons temptingly each and every springtime. This garden draws people from all corners of the earth, who come here to find a paradise of flowering bulbs surrounded by waterfalls, splendid shrubs and woodlands.

Deep winter in the bulb fields. The
bulbs planted in the autumn lie
ensconsed in the earth, safely covere[d]
by a bed of straw. Since there is littl[e]
to do in the fields, this is a period of
happy relaxation for the inhabitants:
like skating or ice-yachting on the
Kager-lake near Warmond.

Come rain or sunshine, on the last Saturday of April the famous flower-float takes place in the bulb area. A festive parade of brilliant floral floats, created with millions of flowers, glide gracefully along a track of some 40 kilometers.

Paintings

Directly behind the line of dunes which serves to protect the low lands from the moods of the North Sea, lies the bulb-growing region. It is a part of Holland which greatly appeals to the imagination. A landscape which deserves to be framed as a painting, is a compliment frequently heard. There, on land reclaimed from the sea centuries ago, millions of tulips, hyacinths and narcissus stand in bloom every spring. It is a fascinating show which throughout the ages has drawn vast numbers of visitors to this area.

Among the multitudes there has also been quite a smattering of artists inspired by the splendid and striking play of colour which natures stages here in the springtime.

Some of the products born of this inspiration are illustrated further on in this book. The compilers did not merely go in search of paintings of the bulb-growing area in the possession of private collectors and museums here, indeed a good deal of investigation was undertaken abroad. America, for instance, was a rather obvious choice since in the final decade of the last century, many young American painters came across to the European continent.

There were **Charles Paul Gruppe** (1860-1940), **Walter Mac Ewen** (1860-1943), **Robert Blum** (1857-1903) and of course, **George Hitchcock** (1850-1913), who of all American painters, produced the most paintings of the bulblands and of whose work a number of examples have been reproduced in this book.

In August 1887 in the American Scribers Magazine, he lyrically described 'the picturesque quality of Holland'. Hitchcock was very much under the spell of 'the sea and its chiefest charm, the atmosphere'. Holland, he wrote, 'is the most harmonious of all countries, both in sunlight and in shadow'.

The light is often very bright, as bright as sunshine. The shadows are never the glaring, violet spots of the southern sun, never is the blue of the skies metallic. The light is always diffused, even in the shadows. And no matter how sharp the sunlight is, the tone is always fine.

In Egmond-aan-Zee, a fishing village on the coast

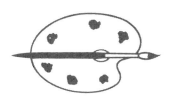

of the North Sea, **George Hitchcock** had a studio, which he shared with a compatriot and fellow-painter, **Gari Melchers**.

The moment the first signs of spring manifested themselves, Hitchcock ritually left his temporary home to go and revil in the exuberant colours of the bulb fields.

Hitchcock was clearly inspired by the Dutch painters of the socalled Hague School, which between 1870 and 1900 made a name for itself, and for style was compared to the French impressionists, especially **Claude Monet** and **Pierre Auguste Renoir**.

The impressionists preferably presented illusions rather than reality on their canvasses. One of the characteristics of their style of painting was the use of loose brushwork, a technique that deviated somewhat from the traditional techniques which were taught at art colleges.

Hitchcock was nicknamed, 'painter of the light'. His work was known for its profusion of colours, which certainly is very apparent in his pictures of the bulb region. He enjoyed painting the farm women, dressed in their costumes and often working in the midst of the flowering fields.

Every artist sees the extravagantly coloured fields in an individual way. This was also the case with the French impressionist, Monet, who worked creatively in the bulb-growing region for a far shorter period than Hitchcock. Still, his sojourn was extremely productive and when he took the train back to France, he was carrying five (still wet) paintings of the bulb fields.

Monet did not set out for Holland on 27th April 1886 on his own accord, by the way. He came at the invitation of Baron l'Estournel de Constant, embassy secretary of the French delegation in The Hague. They were complete strangers to each other but the high ranking official was an admirer of Monet's and he insisted that together they should visit the bulb fields.

Was Monet impressed with what he saw there? He found the bulb fields quite lovely, he wrote to a friend, but very hard to paint because they formed

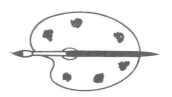

clearly defined surfaces of colour, which were difficult to reproduce harmoniously.

But Monet's genius was undeniable and resulted in five outstanding paintings, two of which are in American ownership, two hang in France and number five belongs to a Dutch museum.

Monet who had the habit of painting beneath a white umbrella, was blessed with good weather. The Dutch climate is rather freakish. In the period when the tulips, narcissus and hyacinths bloom, beautiful, sunny days may alternate with harsh weather, even snow and hailstorms. Monet enjoyed a period of twelve days of stable weather; little wind and cloudy with a ray of sun every now and then.

Many of the artists of whose work one or more paintings are shown in this book, were only casually interested in the bulb-growing region. This was also true for **Vincent van Gogh** (1853-1890) who during his lifetime produced close to 2100 drawings, sketches and paintings but only once in 1883 painted the bulb fields in the midst of somber looking little houses. The picture naturally has been in-

cluded in this publication together with other fine examples of characteristic landscape painting such as that of **Ferdinand Hart Nibbrig** (1866-1915) and **Gerrit Willem Dijsselhof** (1866-1924) who became internationally renowned because of his paintings of fish tanks and aquariums.

Dijsselhof was born in the bulb-growing region but limited himself to only a few paintings of the area, which confirms the popular theory that people are often blind to the beauty immediately around them. In the springtime the perfectly straight rows of bulbs cover the flat landscape beyond the dunes and every artist has given his own interpretation of this sight.

Anton Koster (1859-1931), the most productive artist when it came to painting the bulb fields, captured the fields in some of his work just as they are in reality (rigid, bright lanes of colour). At other times he chose a more imaginative portrayal of the lavish blossoming.

Monet saw this landscape in quite a different light as is evident from painting number 53. The fields

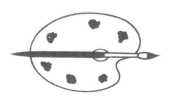

are depicted in a thick pasty layer of paint on the canvas and, in a most wonderful way, exude their characteristic power of light and colour.

In this painting, Monet makes fun of the laws of natural perspective by not fading out the colour intensity towards the horizon, as is usual. Instead the fields in the distance, directly behind the dunes, are just as brightly hued as they are in the foreground. This·is a masterpiece and so is the picture of the bulb fields by **Jan Toorop** (1858-1928), number 17. He went for the pointillistic approach, a style of painting in which the colours are put onto the canvas in tiny dots of paint, which do not merge into each other but still somehow form a complete whole. Various styles and techniques have been combined in this book. The oil paintings are given priority but in addition you will find a few examples of work done in tempera, watercolours mixed with egg white, gum and glue. The artist who works in this medium, **Marjolijn Juray** (1945) has made a name for herself internationally with her speciality: the tulip in the landscape (number 37).

Johan Jeuken (1909-1982) belongs to a movement in the field of painting, which has only won recognition in the last decade: the 'naives' (number 13). These painters have no inclination to present subjects true-to-life but rather dedicate themselves to the spontaneity of painting where the use of primary colours and surprising combinations comes first. The naive painter has a natural candour and is not inhibited by academic or other painting techniques. Perspective and the theory of colour, for example, are of secondary importance to these artists.

In springtime millions of people flock to the bulb-growing region to witness the colourful fairytale for themselves.

Yet there is little or no bustle in the pictures in this book because the painters of the bulblands have something in common with other landscape artists. They prefer peaceful places where they can work hard but quietly. And in the bulb-growing region, many such places still exist. Enjoy these inspired works; each and every one is a masterpiece worth framing.

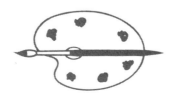

Claude Monet (1840-1926)

Tulip-field in Holland

Oil on canvas, 21x32 inch
Musée Marmottan, Paris.

2 George Hitchcock (1850-1913)

Holland, Hyacinth Garden

Oil on canvas, 17x21,75 inch
Bowdoin College Museum of Art,
Maine.

3 Joseph Raphael (1872-1950)

Tulip-field, Holland, 1913

Oil on canvas, 29x29 inch
Stanford University Museum of Art,
Stanford.

4 Daniël Noteboom

In full bloom

Oil on canvas
Art shop 't Grachthuisje, Lisse.

Jean-Léon Gérome

The duel with the tulip

Oil on canvas
Walters Art Gallery, Baltimore.

6 Bernardus P. Viegers (1886-1947)

Bulb-field

Oil on canvas, 16x23,5 inch
From Polak art-dealers collection,
The Hague.

George Hitchcock (1850-1913)

Flowergirl in Holland, 1887

Oil on canvas, 31x58 inch
The Art Institute of Chicago,
Potter Palmer Collection.

8 Anton L. Koster (1859-193

Pastel, 11x17 inch
Private collection.

9 Vincent van Gogh (1853-1890)

Flowerbeds in Holland

Oil on canvas, 19x26 inch
National Gallery of Art,
Washington,
Collection Mr. and Mrs. Paul Mellon

10 Unknown master

Still-life with bulb flower.

Oil on panel, 22,5x16 inc[

Museum Flehite, Amersfoo[

1 Gerrit W. Dijsselhof (1866-1924)

Tulip-fields

Oil on canvas
DKV, The Hague, on loan from
Dutch Embassy in Lima.

12 Anton L. Koster (1859-1931)

Tulip-fields

Oil on canvas
Private collection.

13 Johan Jeuken (1909-1982)

The Bulb coach

Oil on canvas
Private collection.

14 Adriaan C. van Noort (1914)

Oil on panel, 12x16 inch
Private collection.

Floris Verster (1861-1927)

Lilac tulips in glass jug

Oil on canvas, 13,5x9,5 inch
Stedelijk Museum De Lakenhal,
Leiden.

16 Pieter Korsuize (1907-1961

Oil on canvas
Private collection.

17 Jan Toorop (1858-1928)

Bulb-fields near Oegstgeest

Oil on canvas, 25x30 inch
Gemeentemuseum, The Hague.

18 Willem A. Wassenaar

Bulb-fields near Katwijk

Water colour
Private collection.

19 Anton L. Koster (1859-1931)

Workers in the fields

Ex-collection Art shop Polak,
The Hague.

20 Cees van der Berg (1935)

Bulb-fields

Oil on canvas on panel, 15,5x24 inc
Private collection.

1 Jan S. Knikker jr.

Oil on panel, 8,5x6 inch
Private collection.

22 Anton L. Koster (1859-1931)

Pastel, 11x17 inch
Private collection.

3 Anton L. Koster (1859-1931)

Water colour
Private collection.

24 Wendelien Schönfeld
(1950)

Intercity 111

Woodcut, 10x11,5 inch
Galerie de Witte Voet, Amsterdam.

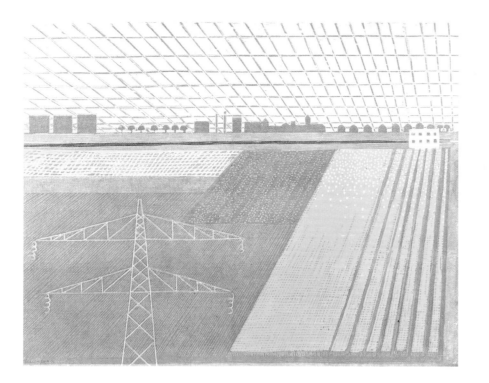
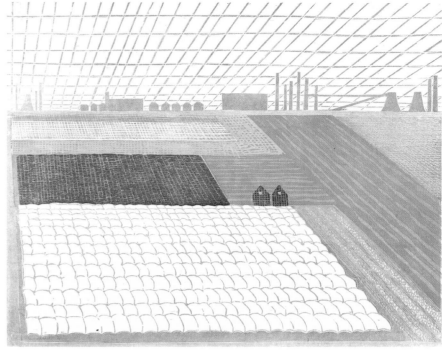

25 Wendelien Schönfeld
(1950)

Bulb-area

Woodcut, 4x (19x22,5 inch)
Galerie de Witte Voet, Amsterdam.

26 Anton L. Koster (1859-1931)

Oil on canvas
Private collection.

27 Hendrik Koster

Bulb-fields along the dunes

Oil on canvas
Art shop 't Grachthuisje, Lisse.

28 Pieter Korsuize (1907-1961

Oil on canvas, 11,5x23,5 inch
Private collection.

9 Ferdinand Hart Nibbrig
(1866-1915)

Bulb-fields

Oil on canvas on panel, 20x28 inch
Singermuseum, Laren.

30 Adriaan C. van Noort (1914)

Oil on panel, 11,5x15,5 inch
Private collection.

**1 Arend Jan van Driesten
(1878-1969)**

Bulb-fields

Oil on panel, 12x18,5 inch
Stedelijk Museum De Lakenhal,
Leiden.

32 Arnoud van Gilst (1898-1981)

Bulb-fields

Oil on canvas, 19,5x27,5 inch
Private collection.

3 Gari Melchers

Water colour, 14x10 inch
A. J. Phelan, Maryland.

34 Anton L. Koster (1859-193

In full bloom

Oil on canvas
Private collection.

**5 Ferdinand Hart Nibbrig
(1866-1915)**

Bulb-fields

Oil on canvas on panel, 15,5x23,5
inch
Stedelijk Museum, Amsterdam.

36 Anton L. Koster (1859-1931

Oil on canvas
Private collection.

37 a Marjolijn Juray (1945)

Tulip landscape

Distemper, 5x9 inch
Private collection.

b Marjolijn Juray (1945)

Tulip landscape

Distemper, 5x5,5 inch
Private collection.

c Marjolijn Juray (1945)

Tulip landscape

Distemper, 12x14,5 inch
Private collection.

38 Anton L. Koster (1859-1931

Barge with hyacinths

Oil on canvas, 11,5x15,5 inch
Private collection.

9 Arnoud van Gilst (1898-1981)

Oil on canvas, 19,5x27,5 inch
Private collection.

40 Anton L. Koster (1859-1931

Tulip-fields with mayflower in blossom

Pastel, 17,5x13,5 inch
Private collection.

41 J. Pasman

Oil on canvas
Art shop 't Grachthuisje, Lisse.

42 Anton L. Koster (1859-1931)

Flowers on trash heap

Oil on canvas, 19,5x27,5 inch
Private collection.

3 George Hitchcock (1850-1913)

In Brabant

Oil on canvas
Los Angeles County Museum of Art,
Los Angeles.

44 a Domien van Baalen
(1952)

Water colour, 19,5x25,5 inc[
Private collection.

44 b Domien van Baalen
(1952)

Water colour, 19,5x25,5 inc[
Private collection.

45 Anton L. Koster (1859-1931)

Rijnsburg

Oil on canvas
Teylersmuseum, Haarlem.

46 Pieter Korsuize (1907-1961

Oil on canvas
Private collection.

47 Frank S. Herrmann
(1866-1942)

Oil on canvas, 27x56 inch
A. J. Phelan, Maryland.

48 Adriaan C. van Noort
(1914)

Oil on canvas, 11,5x15,5 inch
Private collection.

49 Ferdinand Hart Nibbrig
(1866-1915)

Bulb-field worker

Oil on canvas
Private collection.

**50 Bernardus P. Viegers
(1886-1947)**

Bulb-fields in blossom

Oil on canvas
Private collection.

1 George Hitchcock
(1850-1931)

Tulip seller

Oil on canvas, 33x24 inch
Jordan Volpe Gallery, New York.

52 Claude Monet (1840-1926)

Tulip-fields at Sassenheim near Leiden

Oil on canvas, 23,5x28,5 inch
Stirling and Francine Clark Art
Institute, Massachusetts.

53 Claude Monet (1840-1926)

*Bulb-fields and windmills near
Rijnsburg*

Oil on canvas, 25,5x31,5 inch
Public service Beeldende Kunst,
The Hague, on loan from Stedelijk
Museum, Amsterdam.

Acknowledgements

The publishers would like to thank the following for their pictures:

Foto Aerocarto, Amsterdam
Foto Aerophoto, Amsterdam
Foto King Air, Bergen op Zoom
H.N.T. Koster, Keukenhof, Lisse
Foto B. v.d. Lans, Hillegom
Internationaal Bloembollencentrum, Hillegom
B. Ransijn, Sassenheim
P. v.d. Voort, Lisse
H. v. Amsterdam, Sassenheim
J. Hardenberg, Sassenheim
Arnoud Overbeeke, Amsterdam

Acknowledgements

The publishers wish to acknowledge the assistance provided by the museums, archives and owners of the paintings in this book.

The authors would like to thank Mary Anne Goley, Director Fine Arts Program of the Federal Reserve Board in Washington, for her assistance in finding american artists who painted the Bollenstreek.

Design: Peter van der Voort
Lithograph: Reproscan bv, Meppel
Printing: Drukkerij ten Brink Meppel bv
Binding: Koppelman bv, Utrecht

ISBN 90 366 0139 8